Migrant Brothers

Yale UNIVERSITY PRESS NEW HAVEN AND LONDON

Migrant Brothers

A Poet's Declaration
of Human Dignity

Patrick Chamoiseau

Translated by Matthew Amos
and Fredrik Rönnbäck

Yale University Press books may be purchased in quantity for educational, business, or promotional use. For information, please e-mail sales.press@yale .edu (U.S. office) or sales@yaleup.co.uk (U.K. office).

Printed in the United States of America.

Library of Congress Control Number: 2017958971
ISBN 978-0-300-23294-3 (paper : alk. paper)

A catalogue record for this book is available from the British Library.

This paper meets the requirements of ANSI/NISO Z39.48–1992 (Permanence of Paper).

10 9 8 7 6 5 4 3 2 1

For
Hind Meddeb,
Jane Sautière,
Laetitia Fernandez,
Yasmina Ho-You-Fat-Deslauriers

And for
René de Ceccatty

This something that appeared ten or so years ago,
we'll call it the "disappearance of fireflies."
 —*Pier Paolo Pasolini, 1975, shortly before his death*

They don't know that their desire carries so far, into
the great night that imprisons them.
 —*Antoine de Saint-Exupéry*

Do not lose hope in fireflies.
 —*Aimé Césaire*

We must then ourselves—standing back from reign
and glory, in the open breach between the past and
the future—become fireflies and thereby form anew a
community of desire, a radiant, dancing community
despite it all, of thoughts to be passed on.
 —*Georges Didi-Huberman*

Contents

Preface to the English Edition: For a Global Hospitality

This book was born of an encounter in Paris. I had been invited to dinner by some of my friends. Not for the sole pleasure of seeing one another, but so that they might alert me to what was happening on the outskirts of the City of Lights. These friends are artists, actors, journalists, activists . . . They write in the press, perform on stages, film things in impossible places. They are in essence what I am not: people of action.

For months they had been battling on the most unexpected of front lines. Hundreds of people—who had overcome deserts, oceans, walls, lines of barbed wire, checkpoints, who had survived nightmarish camps—were arriving in tireless waves only to crash against police violence in the very heart of Paris. They told me what they were experiencing: tales of daily assistance, accounts of brutality, medical care to be

dispensed, endless steps to be taken in administrative
dead ends. All of which was supplemented by photos
and videos salvaged from their confrontations. They
filled me with a mixture of guilt and silent indignation.

My friends, women of action, exhorted me to write
in my own way about what was happening. By nature
calm, rather contemplative, removed from activism,
I always feel somewhat guilty in front of people who
know how to act, and who act. Even if literature has
often showed me the contrary, it's rare for me to think
straightaway that writing, when the emergency is
under way, could turn out to be at all useful. Édouard
Glissant thought differently. Every time we would
write against something we considered unacceptable,
he would be the one who initiated it. With vigilant
serenity, he thought that beneath the facts, beneath the
horror, a poetic vision was able to identify the forces
at work, and among them to discern *the acting power*
that alone, in the end, would be the key to a decisive
response. Every act, he would say, was born of a poetics. Thus, poetics would usher in politics. My friends
had reminded me, probably without knowing it, of
Glissant's thoughts.

The indignation they had managed to arouse in me hardened into a sort of obsession. What I knew or what I had sensed for months about the terrible migratory phenomenon became one of those particular torments which I can escape only through writing. I found it unbearable that in the Mediterranean, in the full light of day, thousands of people had already lost their lives. That in the coming months and years thousands of others were going to die, in the same places, in identical conditions, and in much larger numbers. That such a slaughter is possible in the twenty-first century, that we can simply tolerate the idea of it, accept the existence of it, can mean only one thing: a barbaric night has settled on the global conscience, and it no longer fears to show itself in the open and without shame. Many are those who say, "Why should we care about this Mediterranean business! It's Europe's problem! If there's barbarity, it's only a European barbarity, it doesn't concern us!" And many are those who retreat into the cocoon of good conscience.

And yet a quick look around the world—the Americas, Africa, Asia, Europe, and their archipelagoes—is enough to show us that migratory phenomena palpitate, persist, insist, convulse in one place, flare up in another. Everywhere, to various degrees, children, women, men who want to move are ground up in lawless spaces in which human beings become strangers to humanity. Borders are sharpened more and more like the blade of a guillotine. Around them, those who come as humans toward other humans, whose only crime is to be human and call out to their brothers and sisters from the depths of a very human distress, find themselves faced with systems which no longer know how to recognize a human being. As if those who ask for help were a breed of medusae that could be blotted out from the face of the earth. A quick look around shows us that this matter is one of the forces at work in the world, and even worse: that it risks becoming one of the major issues of our planet.

Our immediate future will be dominated by two formidable monsters:

1. Climate change.

2. The triumph of neoliberalism, and of its multi-dimensional perverse effects.

Two catastrophes that will lead to ecological up-
heaval, devastating pollution, nuclear accidents, re-
actionary wars, global precarity, and medieval misery
. . . Populations affected in one way or another will
not fail to rush off from wherever to wherever. These
migratory impulses will only intensify. They will be
transglobal but also transnational—but also intrana-
tional . . .

Fixity has never existed in cultures, civilizations,
or identities. It has never existed in life. Any one of
us can, in the wake of a fire, a tornado, a tectonic
fury, a job loss, be forced to leave home and ask for
asylum a bit farther along, in his or her own nation or
beyond. All of us risk finding ourselves inflicted with
the conditions forced upon the migrants in the Mediterranean: a nearly systematic destruction as the only
answer to distress. Inhumanity is still part of humanity. But when inhumanity sets itself up as a cogwheel
mechanism it becomes *dishumanity*. In dishumanity the
principle of humanity itself is threatened by a systematic entity. A murderous, cold robotization, lacking
the limitations of affect. The death knell, the famous

death knell, then tolls for all, but, lacking a human audience, it remains inaudible.

Nevertheless, this book is not intended to fill us with guilt or to frighten us with what threatens us all. Acting out of compassion while fearing for oneself is the lowest form of relationship between a conscience and the indecencies of the world. It seems to me that the intensity of these migratory phenomena is such that they were not simply fed by fear, suffering, and wars. That there is, underneath, *another imaginary of the world.* A particular vision that the exceptional energy of these people secretly possessed. I had to find this power and allow it to project all action beyond humanitarian compassion or fear for oneself. So I attempted to apply to these phenomena the particular poetics that Glissant called globality.

Capitalist economic globalization is not the only force behind the unification of the world. In reality, in this capitalist expansion of the Market, of its alleged invisible regulations, there is no unification. Only the setting up of different places of marketable standardizations that allow the circulation of merchandise and the accumulation of obscene profits. The unprecedented multiplication of contacts, encounters, and exchanges, technoscientific acceleration, and the setting up of an omnipotent digital ecosystem have this as their only goal: markets, profits, financial hoards. And yet, beneath this commercial scheming an encounter between the imaginaries of peoples and individuals is taking place. Truly human sensibilities open up to greater spaces, and, mixing with one another, come together, pass through each other or unite, sometimes fight each other as much as they mutually inform one another. A perception of the world broader than that of our nation alone develops and produces to various degrees, in each of us, the vague consciousness of a world totality: of a world perceived as an indivisible whole. This is globality.

We live not in a state, a nation, a federation or confederation, surely not in a constellation of commercial hyper-places and financial centers, but in an ecological and human totality: extremely reactive, sensitive, unpredictable. It brings us tightly together in a shared fate. All of us together must think and construct this ultimate and grandiose level of the "common good." Not in the desert of haughty, warlike, or arrogant

solitudes, but in the oxygenated luxuriance of encounters, of a mobility in which differences are present, of
a solidary exchange that makes everyone grow, and
of a human competence that in all circumstances will
retain its aptitude to recognize humanity, wherever it
might go, wherever it might come from.

This book pleads for a *global politics of hospitality* that states once and for all, in the name of all,
for all, that in no place in this world, for whatever
reason, will there be such a thing as a foreigner. It is
written to be played, read, sung, listened to, recited,
given to dance and music; its language is made up of
rumblings, sounds, and music, and this allows us to
dismiss from the start economic assessments, efficient
robotizations, and their unblinkingly disenchanted
visions of the world.

La Favorite, October 2017

Migrant Brothers

ind, the one filming, says to me: In France, the Mediterranean is at the corner of the street and the Calais jungle, destroyed by shovels, keeps popping up along the boulevards! . . .

Jane, the one writing, whispers to me: In Paris, I serve hot coffee, slices of buttered bread, to eyes lacking eyelids. The pupils, whitened by vigilance and the salt of deserts, are like semaphores. In the shadow of these bodies that spring up from nowhere, who do nothing but emerge, evanescent between banks and shores, I see roads become eternal, tombs heaped between islands and continents, a vast array of origins that end up jumbled together on a raft of bundles and suitcases . . . Each one of these silhouettes seems to draw its endurance from a burden of tomorrows shouldered without fatigue, carried without future . . .

She sighs to me too: See how destinations are kept

alight like embers, although no one ever arrives at them; how so many little people—children!—can be born into strange solitudes, congenital dagos, spontaneously stateless, untouchables and immanent pariahs, stripped of all sense of belonging, handed over to the damnations of a decree of medusae and sunken boats! . . .

Hind, the one filming, further proclaims to me: In Paris, in Ventimiglia, just as in the Calais region for almost fifteen years, migrants have remained stranded on the margin of all margins, minors are treated like industrial livestock, even rounded up on the threshold of France, land of asylum, and hope itself is rooted out!

They are *tarnished!* . . .

. . . from police stations to detention centers, from detention centers to packages addressed to nowhere, without recourse, without witnesses, without lawyers, often without interpreters, their only asset the per-sistence of a fear that never gives up, that gives up on nothing! . . . Squats are evacuated without anyone caring for the sick, women, and children! The com-passionate are brought before the courts for the crime

of solidarity! Demonstrations are crushed even before
they are risked! . . .

Here, close by (almost so far away), they are
dispersed, they are punished with arrests, rocks are
stacked and barriers raised in spaces dedicated to their
final weariness; over there, far away (almost so close),
coast guards, wall guards, border guards—*guards
of life, guards of death!*—are sick of not being able
to contain them! . . . The flow has the vitality of a
biblical beginning, it swells having never begun, it
begins again having never slowed down and even before it had time to stop . . . At times, guards of misery
machine-gun madly and randomly, and often torture
out of exasperation, and when they find themselves
driven to the limits of their own conscience they cry
without really understanding why! . . .

She then growls with all her youth: *Islamophobia
insecurity identity immigration . . . are words that
have turned monstrous!* They've mated under media
hypnosis, in a shrill horde, and they grind madly like
cogs, in almost every direction, everywhere, almost
endlessly, crushing people under bright city lights

and boulevard garlands! . . . We have to act, here's a cause! . . .

Suddenly, Jane, the one who writes so well, says in astonishment: I saw their eyes, they're fireflies . . .

Yes, in this night, on this raft, beneath this frozen horizon, among these shivering shelters, camps, and bivouacs, destroyed again and again yet always reconstructed, in Europe, but also in Asia, in Africa, in the lands of the Caribbean and the other Americas, what you say, my dears, triggers in the geographies of the wind, in sparks of salt, in sparks of sky, a strange meeting of poets and great human beings . . .

What is it then to act or to make an effort beyond emergency without neglecting the emergency or missing the essential, and without considering that at the origin of this drama reign invisible forces?

And yet how can we not see them? Neo-liberalism nearing triumph; its financial markets lapsed into lethal hysteria; politics deserting within democracies that have become erratic; a state that is dwindling, leaving the economists alone at the helm and bent beneath the weight of innumerable diffuse mercantile entities participating in the fabric of the world. Not a single computer program, not a single screen, not a single innovation in nanoscience and biotech, not a stitch of the mind, and not a single connection escapes their dogma! . . . And here's what this planetary darkening causes: exclusion, rejection, violence, stupidity,

hatred, and indecency fermenting everywhere, inten-
sifying in loops of algorithms and social networks,
exploding in the impulsive horde of the media that
are so fascinated by these networks that they become
mimetic. This collapse leads to a loss of ethics, and
when ethics fail, beauty falls. Pier Paolo Pasolini was
right to be troubled in the face of an Italian night that
seemed triumphant. A similar night is swallowing
us, without alarm, imperceptible, invisible, until
suddenly it is malevolently embodied under a blond
swath of hair in command of the most powerful
nation on earth . . .

Visible Death

But let's leave the invisible and stay with what you can see, in this crepuscular moment, just as for years, as from year to year, for years to come, people, thousands of people, not medusae or bunches of yellow seaweed but people, small large old all types of people, who waste away and perish, and will continue to die for a long time in border garrotes, on the edge of nations, cities, and the rule of law . . .

Europe's borders are set up like mauve arrow slits. They feed one of Dante's infernos and bring back a version of the Abyss that Édouard Glissant spoke of. An Abyss of drowned lives, of fixed open eyelids, of beaches where bodies pulled out of the depths stir up spume. An Abyss of children adrift, asleep in a coral mold, swallowed by the sand or softly disjointed by impassive swells.

Here, Lampedusa, half rock, half torch, half oyster,

almost stellar, which inhales and digests without
space and without time a living substance, and with it
the cobalt blue of the world, its flaxen honor, its green
decency, the suns of its consciousness, too.

Over there, red, the island of Malta, which sees
itself surrounded by terrifying crowns, rings of surviv-
als, a tempestuous wave of hearts, hopes piled high in
spume on closed horizons.

Along the edges of Greece and Italy—whites
torn apart on helpless grays—people, not rocks, not
plastic mesh, people, thousands of people pressed
piled packed together in a sticky lacework in which
the stitches of death and life can no longer be told
apart and are held together in shivering rags of a rich
scarlet mauve, one inside the other.

Screams inhabit the secret nuances of the wind.
Black rafts populate the black swells. Moans adrift,
black as soot, find nowhere to repose, to oppose.
Swirling pains are endlessly repeated, from wreckage
to dead ends, on all possible forms, signed, authorized
and . . . forgotten! regarding access to refuge, requests
for asylum and so-called human rights.

Iraq Syria Eritrea Afghanistan Sudan Libya . . .

are open arteries. Spurts of fixed iridescent violet as if
from deep within a forge. What is bleeding, these pul-
sating swells pouring out—I'm talking about people,
I'm talking about persons—bleeds from us, bleeds
toward us, among us, bleeds for all. The continent of
the Africans from the bottom of the Atlantic—a continent without address, where the holds of the slave
ship for centuries managed to grind the foundations of
Africa, humanity's firstborn—joins its double in the
Mediterranean in an exact sideration. Icy blue, forgotten by clarities! It's like a collective hiccup, a spasm
of our histories, probably a vomiting—in fact, a truly
new beginning, not of the same but of the readmitted
forces of horror.

Neo-Liberal Peace

In the human person, barbarity is natural, a background color, either very cold or very hot, sepia or manganese carmine; we weary of it yet we must forever worry about it, we pass through it yet we never surpass it. It is and will forever be within us, lunar solar, solid and available, and forever of an involutional length right in front of us.

Voluntarily naive, resolutely innocent, still reluctant to awaken to foundational bitterness, we thought the most archaic was far behind us: ancestral violence, whitewash of mystical sacrifices, tribal savagery, fervent inquisitions, a bloody summary of conquest and domination, slave trade, slavery and colonization (which recapitulated each attack on the human race so as to better concentrate and prophesy them all), warring homelands, global conflicts, Nazi camps of acid and embers, leap-year Gulags, rectifying cultural revolutions, genocides that go beyond their proper definition . . . murderous practices inscribed as so many relics in the crimson history of the victors and in the sometimes terrifying legitimacy of those who resisted and resist them still . . . Behind us, archaic violence! Behind us! . . .

Some even lauded the virtues of this capitalist empire where the peace of free trade was offered. We saw them sanctify the order of the Great Market, justify the frenzies of finance and its banks, and agree that a life—our entire existence!—can be reduced to the fascine of overflowing Shopping Carts and "purchasing power." They sang the praises of parochial quietude where desire is sublimated in what we consume, is realized and unrealized, is thereby exhausted without ever burning out, like a persistence hostile to the future.

Of course, barbaric archaisms still arose: colonial persistence without colonization, poorly decolonized fossilized fantasies, blind drone killings that no longer distinguish between war and policing, state executions, collateral atrocities, ethnic cleansings, people's springs crushed by steel-gray winters, Israeli impuni-

ties, the despairs of Palestine, dictatorships expert in
chemical weapons and placed as ramparts against the
Islamist hypnosis . . . and now the madness of terrorism resulting from them like aftershocks, fed
by the plenary session of Islamophobia, its servile
echoes and its racist sources . . . These could only
be marginal spasms! They must not, could not make
us forget that we were at peace! That we had, so to
speak, reached an unalterable degree of serenity,
perhaps even, under the iron rule of the West, the
achievement of "civilization." That we could come
and go, democratize at will, philosophize profoundly
between small sips of beer, make cinema for festivals,
novels for awards, mind-numbing tourism, inoffen-
sive and self-satisfied cultural consumption. That
we really couldn't complain and that barbaric times
were long gone. This indisputable success allowed
us to marginalize these eruptions (sharp and bright
like oxide and cadmium) that would appear here
and there, insist, persist, culminate in brutalities in
Lampedusa Malta Sudan Eritrea Libya . . . in Syria,
where Aleppo, abandoned by all, is now nothing more
than an eternal indictment of all, in the whole of the

Mediterranean, at the closed gates of the European sanctuary . . . These were only anomalies whose shock waves were contained by Frontex and the glorious army of darkness-guards who came forth armed from civilization. It's true that we had . . .

Except that capitalist and financial peace is not Peace. It's the depository of a barbarity that domesticates former barbarities under the arch of "agreeable manners" in which bankers, speculators, and traders cook up their schemes. In the course of its triumph, this barbarity loses its invisibility, as its dungeons appear and its holds overflow, and it finally reveals itself to be as virulent as an old Noah's Ark that would bring together in varying degrees all the virulence that ever existed . . . Oh! May the mass deaths on the Mediterranean open our eyes! May they allow us to distinguish the small everyday deaths, the disaster sown in the foam of our days, the unnamed catastrophe whose *chiquetaille* shadow weighs us down with all its impossibility! . . .

The New Barbarity

Amid urban wealth social alienation is taking hold.
Precarity becomes structural with or without employment. Misery (ordinarily left to ferment discreetly) is
transferred to the somewhat more acceptable domain
of humanitarian compassion. The humanitarian sector
itself sees it as an opportunity to shine anew! It is
no longer assigned to the confines of the Empire, on
the exotic crust of underdevelopment, at the bedside
of those who never managed to enter History. Here
it is, back in the belly of the West, on the bridge in
the sails at the helm at the map at the compass, as
Aimé Césaire would have said. Here it is, in the ruins
of progressive thought, the collapse of the beautiful
socialist dream, at the heart of splendid cities, institutionalized in the leftovers of charitable restaurants and
other food "banks" —veritable shadows of those who,

at the other end of this misery, orchestrate enormous profits.

And now in this wealth regressions arise that eat away at the former status of the employee, at workers' rights, at the cornerstone of the civil servant, at social welfare, at the dignity of those who work their fingers to the bone and produce. The old constellation of labor (I'm talking about a range of different activities in which everyone expressed his or her creativity) is stifled in "employment"—*employment, let's talk about it!* . . . : a prosaic activity, increasingly empty, increasingly mindless, resistant to the slightest accomplishment, until it becomes useless to the robbery of wealth and finds itself transformed into time-limited alms that nothing guarantees and that guarantee nothing . . . If Reason can't do anything about it, may all these dead at least provide us with a fresh pair of eyes, so that we may see!

This misery and other forms of precarity, which don't seem to be connected in any way, are symptoms of the barbarity that we must name: the *paradigm of maximum profit.* Earn big bucks, earn more, earn as much as possible and without reservation! All-profit has become immanent, multiplied by science, technology, and inventions of the digital domain. All of humanity (our prosaic necessities but also our most vital poetic nature) is enslaved to the score of growth points, to the blade of competitiveness, under the emblem of laws in which employment is nothing more than submission to a managerial order nostalgic for feudalism. Research, justice, education, health, culture . . . Penury reigns everywhere except in the exponential dividends paid to shareholders. These miseries, this precariousness, this ransacking of public services, this collapse of solidarity, this alienation that threaten us at the heart of the most advanced of centuries go against the idea inscribed since the beginning in our high moral conscience and that I'd like to kindle here with the following disillusionment: *Wealth, all wealth, no matter what, is created by the work of everyone!*

No manager, no captain of industry, no great business tycoon could separate his or her work from the work of those who carry it, bear it and, in the end, do it. Wealth is produced by all, from lineage to lineage, from family to family, from generation to generation. From a father's or mother's working life to that of a daughter or son who takes over. This is the motor that produces the wealth of the neighborhood, the city, the country—of the world where those to come will be born. This wealth that increases, that is accumulated and concentrated before our eyes in the most extreme, the most absurd fashion, out of the reach of nearly everyone, is nevertheless created by everyone. So it is due to each and every one of us, from the moment of our birth cry. Every birth is naked, fragile, and destitute. Therefore, every birth in this world demands this generosity: acquired wealth, always produced by all, must be distributed equitably and generously, among all and for all! Every birth in its fragility calls for this justice and even orders it.

Liberty, equality, fraternity, sharing, equity, human dignity, and the happiness of all are forces that were established against barbarity. They were able to thwart the triumph of horror. They neutralized reptilian disasters and deflected tragedy arising from immemorial depths. They nourished the "imaginative forces of the Law"[1] and were formalized in Declarations Treatises

---

1. See Mireille Delmas-Marty, *Les forces imaginantes du droit,* vol. 4: *Vers une communauté de valeurs* (Paris: Seuil, 2011).

Charters Conventions Accords and National Codes.
Without ever reaching any sort of completion, these
forces of decency were set up as beacons of a prospect
toward which we are advancing, *by which we are pro-
gressing,* and they protected it from our failings and
resignation. As its victories accumulated, insidious
barbarity (all-profit peace, earning-ever-more, winning-
at-any-cost) was able to make them productively
odious, economically horrible, incongruous with the
arenas of growth and competition. It's finishing up—
and by doing so reveals itself before our eyes—the
pulling apart of these forces stitch by stitch in its raid
on common goods, in its digital ascendancy, in the
consumerist attribution of individuation, in the dis-
credit inflicted on taxes, the state, Politics, and in the
ready-made precarity that is legalized, mandatory, and
proclaimed modern.

The Evidence and the Stakes

Essentially protean, this barbarity was able to spread across the world, to organize the bowls of its dogs until it produced everywhere, in the standard of the same desires, the same futures of consumption, of consumption alone, consumption again, feeding off itself, plunging down lines of flight, attempts at difference, celebrated green solutions, and moderations that we love, which strive to be humble and pretend to be happy.

Nothing human inscribed in life escapes its logic. Nothing can save itself from its crises and ecocides. It connects all our misfortunes and forces us to consider all our challenges together. Everything is connected, everything is tied together! Sterile resistance is above all one that does not know how to link. Therefore banishments, flights, terrors, requests for refuge, pleas for asylum, different circumstances of migrancy should

no longer be separated. All result from the same blow
and stem from the same predation. Sudan, Iraq, Libya,
Syria, Eritrea . . . , same blow, same cause, same present palpitation, and same future!

The planet is not globalized by capitalist appetite
alone. It is by nature one. A single place where the
horizon opens only on itself, where perspective is renewed around a single heart. Multiple worlds perceiv-
ing themselves as autonomous and believing themselves to be impenetrable exist only in the stasis of
our imaginaries. Let's consider this evidence, which
leads to a challenge: a common land, cradle of our
cradles, final nation of our nations, ultimate homeland
where borders are enchanted, a place to understand,
to save, to build, and to live. But also a place for the
time being subjected to the reign of a barbarity as
devastating as any that came before it, everywhere the
same, connected everywhere, and everywhere about
to triumph, as the accomplished empire of all known
and future empires . . .

The Gift of the Knell

Yet, while many poor countries do their best to accommodate mass migrations, the nation-states of Europe prefer to say to life that it shall not pass. They who have migrated so much, shattered so many borders, conquered so much, dominated and still dominate seek to entrench all human miseries terrors and poverties at their place of origin. They claim that the world beyond their borders has nothing to do with their world. That it's not their doing and not their duty. Against it they put up the deterrence of an authorized death, filmed from well-chosen angles, broadcast every day. They raise the proof of impossibility over heaps of corpses and consent to abandoning an entire ocean to the vocation of cemetery. The cradle of their civilization has become a grave. They have tried everything, colluding with infamy—here with the Turkish devil, there with the Greek collapse, later

they abused Italian weakness, and as for the rest they
have populated their shores with mercenary demons.
This is legitimized by economic stability, limits of tol-
erance, security measures against terrorism, national
interest combined with the emptiness of political
pragmatism. They point to identities threatened by
solvent hordes. They say that being out of reach is the
only possible response to what is only the beginning
of an invasion.

Europe considered as alone in the world!

Europe cut off from its own memory, as if born
to itself, feeding off itself, perfected by itself with no
need for Humanity! . . .

And yet, in its very heart, the unforeseeable arises.

Some human beings—I'm talking about ordinary
people, with neither title nor pedigree—awake despite
everything to something within themselves. Like the
migrants, they invent uncompromising paths in anti-
cipation of their own humanity. Without awaiting

any sort of horizon, they take in and welcome shadows specters silhouettes that traverse searchlights and
blinding obstacles. They go toward them, without
a light, without an audience, with nothing but a bit
of trembling humanity. Making themselves both the
audience and the faintest of lights, they give their bed,
their breakfast, their clothes, their time, their solitude
too. *Casa nostra, casa vostra!* Song, dance, music, little
things little gestures little words that probably hold the
tenuous radiance of another world: an intuition that de-
nies dark and powerful truths. *Casa nostra, casa vostra!*

When Humanity is no longer identifiable by humans, barbarity is here. There is not one tribe, not one
nation, not one culture or civilization that hasn't at
some time spread out because of desire or constraint.
That hasn't at some moment of its history seen part of
itself pollinate the world. Or that hasn't welcomed or
been forced to take in something coming from another
end of the world, drawing from the world as much as
giving itself to the world, assuming the role of source of
asylum and refuge, or demanding asylum and refuge.

Not one.

*   *   *

Homo sapiens is also and above all a *Homo migrator.*

Therefore, the man entrenched on his threshold who does not recognize the man coming toward him, who only worries about him, who fears him without letting this fear enrich him, and who would like to see him dead or make him disappear is already dead to himself. He himself has already disappeared from his own memory, from his own history, and in his own eyes. It's himself whom he no longer recognizes. It's his fear of himself that threatens him. It's from himself that he protects himself, and he condemns himself to the shipwreck he fears. In human matters, and in matters of life, the knell knows only all horizons, it tolls from the outset for each and every one, on either side of the walls, beginning with the ringer himself. The retorting gift knows the same scale.

Over There Is in the Here

Jane, you say that they who have become "things" huddle together as if to warm themselves or to make themselves stronger, to live perhaps less alone, probably survive like that, but that the heat that rises from their gatherings hardens the ice in public services, freezes the "gems" of the islets of affluence that our Saint-Exupéry spoke of.[1] You say that all the same this heat breaks down barriers, fills every nook and cranny, but that a police hunt disperses it in a thousand winds and misfortunes, dooms it to impossible extinctions, but that it is reborn even so, disappears only to resurface, neither in the same place nor in the same spot but always in the here, or rather, as we say in Creole: *an mitan isiya!* . . .

1. "Like those thieves of fabled cities, walled in to their treasure chamber which they can leave no more. Among icy gems, they wander, boundlessly rich, but condemned." Antoine de Saint-Exupéry, *Vol de Nuit* (*Night Flight;* Paris: Gallimard, 1931).

I tell her (as well as the frightened man on his doorstep): It's because there is no longer an "Elsewhere." The old barbarities, all recapitulated in the virulence of colonizations, had created non-law, an "Elsewhere" outside the law, non-places, "out-world" places, or, rather, "anti-worlds" where one could at leisure, with clear conscience and impunity and the illusion of non-contamination, terrify, dominate, exploit, massacre, and in the end elevate the dishuman to the level of an institution. The new barbarity erases "Elsewhere" everywhere. Beyond the necessities of its goods alone, it absorbs "Somewhere Else," the resource of any sort of aside. It inadvertently swallows margins and digests distances and differences. By subjecting space to the stripping of its predation alone, it invalidates horizons and always inadvertently creates a tragic unity: the means by which we strike the Other are the same as those that directly harm ourselves. At the moment, under this reign of profit, the suffering-over-there is in the radiant here, the suffering-far-away is near, what happens in any place on the planet seeps into the mist, the clairvoyance and the clairaudience of digital technology, comes together in dusty winds, from loop to loop forms one and the same place. Roads and paths, wherever they begin, wherever they go, only lead back to the place where we are. Affluence that is thought to be isolated and remote in fact nourishes a poverty that sooner or later is going to affect it. Any inequality that is accepted around here or tolerated over there erodes preeminence wherever it might be found. The now very vibratile partitioning of the planet is stirred by the slightest breeze, deplores the slightest cry, stores up the slightest regression—reptilian memories accentuate the impact and fangs remember. The captive scene of the world thus echoes to the four winds all uprootings and bestial quarries. We know without learning, we see without looking, we receive without asking, we hear without pricking our ears, and we take the blow even though it might not be aimed at us. The barbarity that overdetermines the economy, technology, and science turns the world into a place more indivisible than ever by the sheer density of the misery it spreads.

Globality

You tell me, Hind, that one has to see at the break
of dawn the violence of war, dispersals with gas and
truncheons, with cunning and lies, by shame by dis-
grace and by humiliation, in broad daylight, through-
out the cities of Europe, in enlightened Paris, in the
land of an eldest daughter of emancipation! You tell
me that these "things" (reduced to far less than things)
are indignant, incredulous: "But why are you doing
this?!"—and that others remind whoever is able to
hear, sometimes screaming but often in the silence of
burst throats that are their placards, "We are human
beings! . . ."

I say: Their globalization didn't plan for the surge
of humanity. It only planned for consumers. On their
platforms, the human-consumer is not really human
anymore. It's only a simple data point to be filled
with desires, to be covered in services. Stored up

in a cloud of cookies (hypermnesic sticky bees), its
references are auctioned off, its value comes down
to its purchasing power, its presence on this earth
can only be imagined in terms of commercial access
to its digital self . . . No need for this data point to
move about, except as a tourist in the tubing of tour
operators or the entertaining container of immense
ocean liners. And it is preferable that it be demateri-
alized into whatever algorithms and social networks
make of it. Profit has colonized the economy in such
an extremely accomplished manner that the latter has
ended up supplanting the dawn and the horizons, the
alpha and the omega, to the extent of booby-trapping
the lines of flight that virtuality could offer us. In this
night without exit, it's now the economy that *consid-
ers* and grants to people, countries, or what have you
any sort of importance. It dethrones "values," visions,
and grand ideals without having to produce the merest
scrap of an idea. It devours public policy, enslaves
states, accepts in the red ink of its great work only this
end: make more than the day before, always much
more than two days before, constantly grow in order
constantly to accumulate constantly. And why? Not

to reach a certain human propriety—an attention to better living, a concern for well-being—no; to feed a quantitative hypertrophy that is only concerned with itself and threatens our survival on this planet . . . And so, in the heart of this darkness, what was not planned for, what is affirmed on these placards of amygdaloid intensity is that beneath this globalization, like the sublimated trail of a comet, the *globality* that Glissant spoke of opens up.

Submitted to economic dogma, precipitated into the immanence of the digital, the human imaginary registers the uncontrollable irruption of the world. Experiences a consciousness of it. Activates a practice of it. While many of us refuse it and succumb to colonialist nostalgias, to sickly racism, to xenophobic worries, to frenzied extremisms (which is also a miserable way of being in the world), others draw from it a quiet benevolence. From this benevolence, this *glow,* as Pasolini would say, *globality* is born.

Globality is all of humanity seized by the divination of its diversity, connected in expanse and depth all over the planet. In its silent alchemy, globality diffuses within us the presence of something invisible that is vaster than our place, of a part of us that is vaster than ourselves. It amplifies our perceptions, multiplies our points of contact, invents new ones, calls forth the unknown and the unforeseeable in our lives and thus fills us with wonder and throws us into a panic. It inspires in us a taste for learning how to live this unknown and this unforeseeable, how to accommodate them without being bowled over by them, grasp them despite everything. It exudes the intuition of a world that we inhabit, that inhabits us, that we touch and that touches us, that is already constructed but that we can continue to build, that shapes us but in which we can pursue a future. It infuses in us the feeling of a world that is open and that opens us, impossible to fragment, impossible to totalize, impossible to circumscribe, impossible to define, that emerges in shadows in traces in flights in voids in shocks and in lights in strange connections of our imaginaries. A world impossible to conceive but that, because of this impossibility, from the depths of this sovereign fluidity, stimulates the effervescence of creativity. A world where no one is the center or the periphery, neither master nor slave, neither colonist nor colonized, neither elect nor unworthy, where the uncertainty in which we fall reigns alone, both solitary and solidary, equally disarmed, in sensitive expansion and poetic rejuvenation.

Globality is above all what economic globalization did not envisage, arising and occurring on the scale of a glimmering in a dark jumble. It is human unexpectedness—poetically human—that resists them, exceeds them, and refuses to abandon the world! It's what proves to them that the world is not theirs, neither a profit bowl nor a container ship! Their Market connects only the "icy gems" of capital and goods. It clears the way for greed alone. Its contacts are blows, its exchanges are takeovers, its regulations set up nothing but enslavements. Its horizon (where digital profit bubbles bump against one another) is nothing but a totalitarian lid. Therefore, globality is the part of our imaginary that instinctually unravels and thoroughly opens, that instinctually connects to other imaginaries, that rallies that relays and relates sensibilities, joy, dance, music, friendship, encounters, that arises from the magnetisms of these multi-trans-cultural encounters, orchestrated by chance, accidents, luck, and wandering.

Globality is what tilts our ideas of what is human toward the horizontal fullness of what lives on this earth. It is what strives to make this humility the foundation of sharing, and of regulation by a sharing that is not the Market. It sets up none of the economic horizons that seal and confine in order to merchandise us. It unleashes a constellation of intuitions similar to a flight of images, light, somber, green, blue, swirling among themselves, bearing feelings that awaken us, feelings that think, feelings that create, participative feelings and fulgurant ideas that attract one another, repel one another, pass through one another mutually, and thus galvanize one another . . .

This indefinable relationship with the all-living of the world moves us, *affects* us, as the philosophers would have said. It slowly transforms us, without goal or intention. Offers us the experience of more human intensities. Motivates us with something other than the laws of profit and its exclusions. Fills us finally with an ethics lacking in posturing, mindful simply of beauty. Beauty of the immobile. Beauty of nothing. Beauty of the useless and the gratuitous. Beauty of gesture. Beauty of attitude. Beauty of thought. Beauty of every desire and of aspirations . . . of everything that is not in the box with the icy gems! . . .

Globality is what, in the winds of the world, allows us to glimpse other futures toward which we can strive with every fiber of our life and our experience, even before knowing their substance. A world is within them, another world opens within us like a swath of light against the bite of a shadow. A planet is dying of them, an earth offers itself to us that they cannot envisage but that we can acquaint with a poetics they cannot condone. They will not see this world. They will not see us in this world. We will lose sight of them in a swarm of images.[1] So this is what you need to consider: *They drive back migrants because migrants do not leave them the world.* Migrants take it back from them. Sprung from one of the forces of globality, they give it to us in their leaps, in their jumps, with their blood with their dead, with their abundance of life, in winds and waves (*balans*)—with the infinity of the word *W-E-L-C-O-M-E* that they

1. See the exciting conception of the image in Georges Didi-Huberman, *Quand les images prennent position* (Paris: Minuit, 2009).

force us to spell out in all the languages of the world. *Kay mwen sé kay-ou tou!*

This morning, you say, Jane, that you got up early to serve breakfast to "things" that sprang up from a blind spot in the pavement . . . The world is what appears in these scattered tents. The world is what emerges in these humanitarian villages and these dreadful camps. Iraq Eritrea Afghanistan Sudan Libya . . . follow in the wake of goods and services, the sanctified nomadism of securities and capital all along the old colonial scars, with their deep songs, never quite healed. They are suctioned up by interests and profits. By tubing and pipelines that do nothing but vacuum up. The puppets in turn manipulate the string that moves them and force the impulses to move backward. They cling to the bellies of airplanes, to the axles of trucks. Syria takes refuge in the convoy of containers, and in all the corners of the world, justifiably or not, human lines cross snows, rocks, deserts, storms, tear themselves to shreds on barbed wire, assail walls and fences, pile up until they almost touch the sky, and excavate hell. Each one of their steps produces multiform ramparts, lawless

areas, forbidden lands, and red lines, blockhouses set
up as horizons. But each one of their steps is a force,
come from afar, come from another world already
at the heart of this one. All the far-away all that is to
come the future bucking in the right-here itself! With
each of their steps, tell yourself that a force rises from
the heart of the world.[2] Whoever eats with them eats
with the planet's hardiest and in the presence of all.
And whoever serves them serves her own presence
in the unforeseeable connections of the world. That's
why, Jane, this poured coffee, this bread you offered
them, contained this separation: a presence that
recognized their own and joined it in a natural flow.
This presence—I mean this reflection of a beauty that
could have been lost—is nothing other than globality.

They follow not the terrestrial magnetisms that
mobilize animals, not the mere wake of goods, the
musk of capital, the fantasized places where capital-

2. "Whoever walks unfolds the world, / one horizon missed
after the other. / All that remains. / Is a step still a name? / From
now on I belong only to my step. / Light, the word of the
world, / pronounces our passing shadows / and identifies us." In
"The Long Walk," an unpublished poem by Emmanuel Merle.

ism still welcomes workers' arms . . . No. Imagine
this: they also follow the signs of an intuition that
undoes their horizons. Citizens of this globality (which
capitalist geographies will never know), they are
unclassifiable—at the same time clandestine banished
expelled expurgated exiled desolate wayfaring rowdy
refugees expatriated repatriated globalized and de-
globalized, desalinated or drowned, seekers of asylum, seekers of all that the virtues of this world lack,
seekers of another cartography of our humanities![3]

They come with no flag, banner, or coat of arms,
no proclamation other than their humanity reduced
to the ardent expression of its *force of action,* its
power of existing. The chapels they build are filled
with smashed, no doubt creolized, gods. And when
they pray (whether they know it or not), they do it
just above the mud, toward an unfamiliar world of
old sacred texts. Their word their cry is of respect for
Natural Rights, inalienable indivisible, for our humanities. Words that are danced, runs that are sung, cries

3. See the beautiful explorations of Michel Agier in *Les Migrants et Nous: Comprendre Babel* (Paris: CNRS Éditions, 2016).

that are thrown in color on walls, shaken on the bows
of rafts, evoking in their concert what was written on
this subject and now seems erased. They sow Original Rights, Imagined Rights, Ever-Changing Rights,
Rights to Succeed, which they themselves divulge,
which their feet implement, their every cry is a judg-
ment, their every death a precedent. These Rights are
lugged around like so many suitcases, reinforced by
those who fall, transmitted by those who continue,
with great mass and force of will, with nothing but
desire to oppose the damnations of border guards and
other barbed-wire assassins. Against Rules of Law,
they speak on the side of "imaginative forces of the
Law," from the shores of a world where they have
made landfall, which they are already surveying and
that we must construct within us and around us. What we
are (let them march, let them sing, let them scream, let
them die . . . let them illustrate it in this way) is made
up of the world that has changed, that still changes
to the foreign rhythms of globalizations that are—
definitely—the *African polyrhythms of globality.* It
changes us like one of Miles Davis's improvisations,
minutely and soberly, until we realize—*Ah!*—the

unprecedented nature of this change. So this is a part of the task that falls to no one in particular but that stares at us all: To consider the world and the gaping wounds opened by the American kind of slavery, by the blow of colonizations against humankind, but at the same time to make out the molecular future of the world that went on despite everything, above, below, across but also unbeknownst to colonizations; to think of the world to come, of the world we want, of the unforeseeable world, to accompany the inevitable junction of all these worlds within us, to make out their potentialities, to specify without forcing our desires, to identify without pushing the determination that will support each desire, and then to invoke them as an inspiration at every second of an existence that has become confident again—we too must migrate, like this, in the swarms of improvised images that swirl like lights within us!

Certain imaginaries swirl on a daily basis. They come together. Open up sometimes from simply coming together. Lower the shields, push aside the lattice of reptilian roots, are moved by the far-off, broaden the nearby . . . They get a taste of the unknown in the unknown to come. They recognize a brother in the stranger who comes. A family in the mass flights even though nothing human can be distinguished in them. Globality lies then in the misery and pain that come in a convergent drift. It accentuates the unacceptable aspects of their globalization. It is here, it is there. Silent, indisputable, it creates *justice* within us. It creates *equality* within us. It creates in us *decency* and *equity.* It sketches the ethics of another world for us, encourages us to think differently and to let another imaginary go to work. It changes us, and by untangling our dreams accompanies this change. Certain imaginaries dance *fout'* and add colors to their pollution and lead clouds!

This sad expression is coming back: *No one should have to welcome all the misery of the world.* It is nothing but insipidity offered to their indifference. Globality, however, murmurs to us that there is nothing to welcome besides ourselves. The threat does not come from outside of those who speak in this way. It is within them. It keeps to the regions that, in every nation and in each one of us, have become unfit for what remains alive. A Nation does well to rediscover

the ardors that have always presided over its birth.
These encounters, these contacts, these borrowings,
these inter-retro-actions of which it has made history
density and triumph. Nothing was founded in immobility and fixedness. Withdrawal nourishes only life's
dead ends. Living places (that receive, that welcome,
that remain in these first vitalities) are also the ar-
chives of old communities. They irrigate our societies
sprung from the convulsions of the world. *A Nation's
vocation here is to welcome all the misery for which
it is made accountable by its experience, the scope of
its foundation, its historical decency!* Not-very-wealthy
countries have welcomed far more of these unfortu-
nates than certain regions of radiance and affluence.
Indeed, many poor countries that have remained welcoming have assumed a more than optimal responsi-
bility and have set themselves up, if not as examples,
then at the height of what has been most alive within
them and where they desire to remain. To retreat beneath our capacities when distress arises is tantamount
to invalidating our own life, to weakening our future,
to offending the living. *A man screaming is not a
bear dancing!* . . . thundered Césaire. Except, even

a call without howling, a call without questioning, a
just call made of a power of existing in the grinding of
opposite forces does not resonate in the ears alone or
in the sensitivity of the heart: it creates a concert of all
the world's imaginary.

The world and its miseries are regions of ourselves.

To make a country of this world, wealth of these
miseries, they are ours.

To make courage of these fears, they are ours.

To make encounters of these flights and terrors,
they are ours.

To make a minaret of Asylum, a cathedral of Refuge, a temple of Benevolence, they are our dignities.
To apply this expanse to our own affluence, whatever
it may be, whatever it may fear, this is our greatest
challenge. To refuse to look upon what is handed
down from a safety throne, or from the retrenchments
of a treasure island, this is our glory. To organize in

the middle of humanity our irruptions into the irruption of the world, this is our humility. To unlock
everything within ourselves so that we may open
within us a sanctuary for what is human, this is our
freedom. To negotiate thus the crest of an adventure,
already lived by everyone, of which the development
of our conscience retains the memory, this is our way
of staying alive.

Globality reminds us that the world is made up of
ecosystems. Of forces, solitary and together, antagonistic and solidary. An interlacing of differences—
or better yet, of divergences—that are organized in
bonds of repeating equilibriums. This interlacing of
the living says to us, as Hölderlin sang, *Come into
the Open, friend!* . . . It constantly integrates different
situations, frequents the desire for the unfamiliar, the
presence of a mystery, the taste for a difference, the
cool alcohol of a distance, and then of another, works
at swells that make fluid in you and all around you
what is dead what is fixed what is not being born in
unusual ways. Make sure that nothing about the world
seems hostile to you, and everything in the world will
complete your presence, will extend it a bit more,

will keep it alive. Accept this effusion in the alchemy
of distortions to come, which are leaving or coming
back, which produce loads of differences, labile
diversities, in you and for you. With you. And all
around you.

When it reaches its highest degree of relation to
what is, to what's coming, an ecosystem develops
an increased sensibility to differences, tangencies,
and divergences that never cease to assail it. At this
low-water mark of maturation, these become de-
sirable. Enriching and necessary. The ecosystem is
then shaken by the force of the new. Retreats into
separation. Goes toward the unexpected. Opens wide
to the unforeseeable. Initiates the tension of another
togetherness of fluid reinterpretations. A transition is
put in place in which differentiations become radiant,
unleashing the uncertainty of possibilities, the unforeseeable, even the unthinkable of an open future. Keep
intact this always reformative sensibility, which will
give rise to the reflex known as welcome.

What is the cause of these migratory movements?
Of course: war, terror, fear, economic hardship, climate chaos . . . But also: *the secret call of what exists*

differently. Most migrants have identified a place of
arrival that they have chosen or that their perception
of the world has chosen for them. They are inhabited
by a vision sprung from globality. Probably subjec-
tive incomplete biased, alienated by the dominating
forces that format our imaginary, but a vision none-
theless. Within them, it has broken the verticalities
of the landscape, expanded above borders their vital
territory. Set it up in the ardor of a promise. It is this
vision that makes their movement imperial, tensed
between life and death and accepting itself as such.

This vision is an authority.

It does not know how to read any of the old limits.

It knows only how to invent passages, to open ways,
to go with a constancy that remains intact even when
it doesn't reach its goal, that continues thus, tracing
in its unique wake a new geography, open from the
first step, affected in the same instant, that they plow
beforehand with their intuition alone, that they live
before they really know it, that they possess before

even arriving, and that remains all the stronger and more real because it is prohibited. This is the reflection, dear Jane, that you thought you saw shimmer in their eyes.

Globality (which is diffused in us as the totalitarian grip is strengthened) is a relational energy whose intensity is ceaselessly fulfilled. No one could ever, without leaving life behind, go against its swell! It overturns what is dead and activates the future. *Those who do not know how to recognize suns without furor and gods without altar confuse it with globalization. Reject it with globalization, thereby submitting to this very globalization.* Glissant, leaving fixities behind, following the piercing brilliance of a thinking of the Diverse, a philosopher confronting expanse, a poet of the places of the unthinkable, a thinker of the other of thought, in order to refuse to leave them the world would say, *All-World!* as one says, "All-Living!" and saying this was to say, "Relation!"

From the Relational Fact to the Idea of Relation

We must distinguish the relational fact from the idea of Relation. The latter (which Glissant raises to the level of a poetics) is not simply a mobilization of "values" in opposition to the dehumanizations of their world. These values (along the lines of freedom, charity, solidarity, cooperation, equality, fraternity, humanism, et cetera), handled like spare parts, can be instituted as systems—Mother Teresa, they say, was compassionate, tirelessly occupied with misery and poverty, founding her own eternity upon their eternity. The generosity of soup kitchens clears our conscience while at the same time working to maintain something unacceptable. The beautiful idea of liberalism, hastily turned into an economic absolute, is nothing more than a star, foreign to true freedom or to the accomplishments of an individual soul. Humanism set up as a value, vertically erected at the center of existence,

has tolerated many attacks on animal and plant conditions, and, consequently, on that of humanity itself
(often it has sorted them or distinguished between
them, often sorted or distinguished in life as a whole).
Humanism, experienced as preeminence, has kept the
relational fact at the level of a godsend for egocentric
fevers. The relational fact (which no one can escape
in globalization) has neither morals nor superego.
It is as much a place of death, of devastation, and
of domination (slave trade, slavery, colonization,
neo-liberalism, digital paradigm . . .) as a swarm of
surges (resistances, resiliencies, digital amplitudes,
creativities, globality . . .). The relational fact can be
considered as a diagram of reptilian, antagonistic,
and solidary forces, lacking any intention, in which
one can nevertheless make out the infinite relation of
everything to everything, of me to the Other, of order
to disorder, of knowledge to mystery, of the thinkable
to the unthinkable . . . By opening us to globality, by
helping the relational imaginary become intelligent
within us, chaos can become fertile. The relational
imaginary (brought to benevolence) finds the opportunity for a much broader, profounder, and humbler hu-

manism, better in keeping with life . . . The dynamic
that goes from ourselves to the Other, from the Other
toward ourselves, comes out on top, and the notion of
the Other is opened up beyond the mere presence of
humans.

Ultimate otherness becomes the *all-possible.*

In this hotbed of forces, the imaginary moved by
globality nourishes those of mutual aid, of solidarity, of complementarity, of respect for the Other, of
care for a horizontal and radiant fullness of life . . .
In doing so, it works out the mysterious forces that
connect the conceivable to the inconceivable . . . On
this great stage where winds and forces push and pull
from all sides, what is difficult is to stay humble, as
decent, as caring for the Other, as human as possible. Which amounts to constructing a solitude that
deepens you and extends you toward everything. A
poetics of Relation embodies humanism only by the
measure of its humility in the accepted fullness of life.
Thus possibility requires the presence of its opposite.
Knowledge requires the presence of mystery. Nothing

is thinkable unless confronted with the immanence of
the unthinkable. Full life exists only in the open, in
prudence, in care, in decency and in moderation . . .
The much-vaunted "values" are always consubstantial
with a true establishment of Relation.

They are one.

Convergent like torrents in an open valley.

They are all there, right there, together, and thus
neutralize the intensity of anything that would oppose
them. No need to isolate them in mechanical essen-
tializations that can be murderous. If one of them ends
up failing to take part in their interactions, the encounter doesn't take place, the Relation doesn't happen,
and globality remains one of those feelings that dares
nothing and transforms nothing.

Fear and Trust

The relational imaginary makes globality the domain
of conscience. The latter can then without a shield
take up the adventures of living in the fire of life.
This allows it to favor its subtle flavors without fear.
To be initiated into polyrhythms born of differences
when they call to each other and find one another,
often complement one another, sometimes repel one
another, but each one conserves the memory of the
other. Life functions in this way. With neither fixity
nor truth. Nor naive idealism. Simply a relational fact,
imperial and changing. The planet itself was created
in this way, from a relational effusion in which homi-
nization let its epic unfold until it yielded the improbable Sapiens: the fertility of a spiritual clarity that sees
the world, that sees itself in the world, that perceives
its inexhaustible mystery, its innumerable possibilities, that lives the unprecedented and unthinkable, and

then acts, forced to create, against death, against
mysteries, to create, much like life, not necessarily
against but *with* the unthinkable. *All creation arises
from a mystery and presents to us above all a mystery.*
This mystery is to be lived. The beauty of a creation
is linked to the degree of conscience and mystery
that it imparts to our existence. Self-consciousness is
primarily creation, it eludes fixities, it sees the depths
that overwhelm Reason, it knows expanses that only
become deeper, it senses, discerns without defining,
knows without retaining, recognizes without naming,
it goes, endlessly. At first immobile in the mind of
the dreamer, of the sorcerer, of the poet, then in the
leaping desire of the hunter, the energy of the circular
wanderer, finally in the enterprise of the traveler, the
ferocity of the conqueror, the appetite of the merchant
. . . the, alas, protean force of domineering hordes.

This is the lineage from which their globalization
came.

Globality began in an identical way, albeit in the
nuances of sensitivity to the self. It is benevolent in

the mind of the dreamer, ardent in the symbolic extension of the sorcerer, limitless in the wonder-terror
of the mind of the poet, *O essential wound!* It kept
itself going, diffuse like a glow, beneath the reptilian
advancement of nations and peoples, luminescent like
a fog in the clarity of knowledge, and still expands in
the intensities of relational winds. Now that a climax
has been reached, it can fill our imaginaries with
"another region of the world," a different sensibility,
that permeates us (without giving it) with a henceforth
wide-open totality.

Open to what?

To the poetics of a living without conquest and
without domination.

Of an inhabiting given back to great common
spaces.

There is no fixity that does not die.

There is no border that is not crossed.

*   *   *

There is no living reality that does not move and is not constructed in this way.

Sapiens Africanus was born not in a lattice of sharp borders but rather in open ecosystems, punctuated by climates, shortages, abundances, droughts, and floods, ruptures and junctions, alliances, parasitisms, antagonisms, sharing, and exploitation . . . It was familiar with a "Place" that its mystics extended far beyond the narrowness of a territory, beyond the completion of the horizon, beyond the symbolic straitjacket of its first covenants.

A "World-Place" to the energy of which it conformed. It left, ventured perilously. From migrancy to migrancy, Sapiens grew out of the worst and the best, first in extent, then in depth, finally in complexities . . . and then began anew. Its communities became sedentary and lost sight of each other, then found each other again, different and alike, similar and distant. Different in their references to great absolutes, then in a proliferation of separations, divergences, distortions that made them distant in their proximities, nearby despite their distances . . . They forgot each other and found each other again sooner or later, always found each other again, from above, from below, from a distance or from the depths, no matter the axis of the horizon, with strangeness, variations without absolutes, experiences that confront one another until they recognize one another . . . This might summarize a common trajectory in the sequence of tribes, nations, more and more complex empires that crumble and are reconstructed, until the four horizons smash into each other, memories and histories are brought to a boil, great narratives are plunged into a hotbed of images.

The moment!

Our moment.

This development tells us that there is no tumult of separations that does not subside and taste the concert of a new difference, of a renewed separation, enriched by the soul of those who came before, strengthened by the sugar of those who came first, exceeding their own sources, and thus glorifying them.

This was the purloined energy of migrancies.

Not only hunger, fire, thirst, war, climate, water, terror, the marquetry of misery, the abyss of invincible precarities, but the secret song of difference—distortion, divergence—which, reaching a climax, is set in motion toward another difference established as a provision, and itself becoming a provision.

The moment!

The moment of unprecedented migrations!

Migrations laying a new foundation.

The Diverse always becomes organized, that's how it keeps going, from surges to emergences. Difference, separation, distortion are not only a problem for the "same" that settled down, that "identified" itself as such, and from then on cut itself off from life.

Difference (and its declinations, which are creolized, which move away from absolutes and "essences") has its origin only in differences. Its future only in differences. The soundest identity is a trust that opens up and calls out, that thus moves toward change. It's always in a concert of differences that one founds something new and viable for everyone and that one remains in the evolving mystery inherent to life. The world now establishing itself in our full consciousness was made in this way. The ocean of viruses bacteria substances and improbable materials, foam, algae, plants, animals, hominids, the tiny shrub of Sapiens are going to search each other out, cluster together, connect, contort, constantly forming themselves in this total movement. There's no life without movement, no vitality without migrancy—physicochemical migrancies, stellar migrancies, migrancies of genes, migrancies of bodies, migrancies of the spirit and the idea of living, migrancies laying a new foundation for our imaginaries . . .

Neo-liberal barbarity has in its way locked down the world. Defeat would be to think that this lock protects us. There is a resignation in thinking that the old borders depend on the lineage of murderous walls. That, thanks to their garrotes, cultures and civilizations have assured their greatest permanencies. In reality, the old borders, flexible, shifting, often born of arbitrariness and colonial absurdities, have always been animated by a strange poetry, always plagued by their own transgression. They have forever endured the crossing of the new, of life, have reconfigured themselves accordingly. Today, when goods and capital cross, it is not life that crosses, it is the "same" that settles in, uniformity that begins its reign, difference that sputters out into simple variety under the stamp of barcodes and shopping malls. Fixity that takes over and does away with every future apart from trends and consumption. What the border that has become an arrow slit protects, then, is not a difference but rather nothing more than a market, the local turf of a small commercial mob. The examples of Uber Airbnb Google Yahoo Facebook . . . prove that the digital ecosystem is only conditioned by the barbarity of maximum profit. This digital self that captivates us unconditionally is dominated by it. If we do not choose another imaginary for ourselves, between robots, cognitive chips, and screens, we will entirely become its subjects.

Yet the enemy is not digital technology.

It's rather the spirit that for the most part motivates it.

Globality urges that we submit these platforms, these networks to the fulfillment of a social and communal humanity. Where their globalization is going to soak these markets in the dogma of Security (of Public Order governed by an omnipotent police), globality is going to remind us how much better the principle of Safety protects us, without feeding the illusion of an eradicated risk, without giving up the least of our individual rights, without giving up the merest of public freedoms.[1] Civilizations have never closed themselves off from the world. They have always had

1. See Mireille Delmas-Marty, *Les forces imaginantes du droit,* vol. 4: *Vers une communauté de valeurs* (Paris: Seuil, 2011).

a taste for the world in the forever spellbound fear
of the world. They have always endured a tension
between a refusal of the world and an imagining
desire for the other shores of the world. Borders are a
vitality that glistens in these twin forces: the one that
opens, the one that closes. The one that welcomes and
the one that refuses to welcome are within us, on the
same plane, subjected to intensities of fear and trust
triggered by the dawns or twilights of our imaginaries.
Absolutes have never constructed as many wonders as
when great winds howled, and when trust let them be
exposed to these winds even while trembling, and be
nourished by them one way or another.

There is no absolute that has not known the
Diverse.

There is no absolute that hasn't secretly been
enchanted by the Diverse.

The imaginary of Relation can know fear and trust
alike, yet here fear heightens the attention for the
openness of possibilities, and trust gives, gives from

the start, gives without end, gives much more than it receives, and gives while not receiving.

Where their Market should distinguish the best, protect the common interest, it ensures the largest profit, but not for all, for a very small handful. The easiest profit, total and indecent, cut off from social reality, a stranger to ethics, and without known limits. It deregulates in order to make everything conform to this law and leaves individuals alone, workers alone, public and private employees alone, all trans-muted captive consumers, perpetual negotiators of their terms of employment, self-employed deluded by solitary intoxication, who themselves transform their freedom into fuel for the ruling powers. All-profit is this systemic freedom that only enslaves. It's a placing-under-relation that is incapable of any human value. Globality, its relational poetics, throws in the unexpected, and overwhelms the liberal lock with the irruption of humanity and a once more multiform and radiant idea of work.

The lock of the Market is a placing-under-relation teeming with hierarchies, inequalities, human regressions . . . The sensitive Open of globality makes possible a placing-in-relation: a full exchange. Total. A trust in human adventure, its movements, its encounters, its contacts in which the exchange changes us, in which fear only feeds trust, in which cohesion founds an authority that abandons no ethics.

The Relational Ecosystem

I tell Jane: You saw only shadows, coffins, and roads,
and you still offered your cup of coffee . . . She who
brings support to what resembles her is a child of
globality. But whoever does it without worrying about
resemblance is already a poet of Relation.

Welcoming is a reflex, immediate, like a skill of
human sensibility that arises under the impact of the
unknown, of the unforeseeable, a sudden distortion
that overturns the mind, surpasses fear, and mobilizes
benevolent sources and resources. In welcoming, we
take in, then go beyond: *we take care,* get tangled up,
get wrapped up in a shared space. When welcoming is
anticipated, is ruminated, is constructed, is organized,
it becomes hospitality, an established culture of life
that wants to remain alive in full and high conscience
of the Other. If a "clear conscience" can be stupid
and vacuous, high conscience is always between

fear and trust, between tact and audacity; *it trembles* in the sense that Glissant envisaged. When the bud of welcoming begins to bloom into hospitality, high conscience is there, like the spring or like the season in which rain is royal and prolific.

Surpassing itself, welcoming calls for a framework of hospitality that cannot reach fullness without a poetics and politics of Relation.[1]

To be moved by our reflection in the miseries of the Other and to found our compassion thereon, as is often done in the unexamined impulse of welcoming, is a bit like helping ourselves. To be moved above all by ourselves is often a sign that we are failing the world. Relation demands that we live the uncompromising fullness of the gift.

The gift liberates whoever gives and whoever receives.

It does not recognize, it does not oblige.

1. See the call by the Maison des Passages, in Lyon.

*   *   *

It offers the possibility of a relation, elevates and ennobles.

Touched by this fullness, the Other will or will not come toward me. Will help me as he or she wishes. Will carry me from then on more generously and farther than I could ever do. If my helping the Other is carried out in opaque otherness, in perplexing separation, the unknown and even the unknowable, a relational extension takes place: *Any presence in the world will find a place there.* There are so many human beings who do not respect trees or who have no brother among the plants. So many others who have no care for anthropic hells where animals disappear, where planetary biodiversity withers. Today, as mass extinctions are accelerating, every disappearance of a species leads to the loss of hundreds of others, affects the fullness of thousands of others, weakens those that remain. There is not a single presence on the planet that does not suffer as a result of the reign of Sapiens, the principal devastator! Sapiens can show itself to be capable of the highest level of Relation, or ravage it like an infirm murderer of this same Relation. To accept the opacity of the Other, "all the Other," the unpredictability of the Other's choices and true nature, is already to relinquish domination of the Other, domination of "every Other," and therefore domination of the world. It is to make ourselves available for the perception of what the world is, and of the possibility of living in it in the most decent way.

To hold out a coffee and to be able to say: "You are not me, you don't look like me, you will not do what I would like you to do, you are free and opaque as I must be to your eyes, and I give you this whole-heartedly . . ."

Or even: "We do not have a common history, we only have a future that we will no doubt share but that is impossible to foresee, and I give you this whole-heartedly . . ."

*   *   *

True gifts activate the fluctuation of an open future rather than the basis of a past established on sameness. Brothers and sisters, yes, because we are either going to lose ourselves together or become together. By building on becoming we undermine the reproduction of the "same" in which our "common values" prosper. When the "same" is constrained, diversity sings, possibilities are unleashed. A coffee offered to shadows with big eyes is thus not a "value" that one can isolate and fiddle with in a mechanism: *it is a spark of Relation.*

In Relation, no one could or would be able to disappoint anyone else. Help received would not imprison the recipient in any sort of dream, and migrants would not bring those who welcome them into theirs. Gilles Deleuze was afraid of being dragged into someone's dreams. In fact, dreams sometimes generate absolutes that can be murderous. Migrants will be able to go come stay leave disappear return survive or live in a labyrinth of their dreams that will remain unfathomable. The coffee that is offered, the care of which it is the subject will help them galvanize their future as much as that of whoever gives it to them.

Welcoming, here, is not only a gift.

It is one of the modalities of righteous living in the world.[2]

It opens onto a principle of Relation, not onto the hooks of reification. You cannot demand of individual migrants that they become exemplary. In a relational ecosystem, the irruption of a rogue should not result in any sort of collective punishment. You cannot punish rogues more than others under the pretext of having offered them a warm welcome. Those who betray or disappoint only betray themselves, they are sovereign over their own future and they accept their responsibilities. They cannot disappoint your expectations because your only desire—the one you allow

2. See the fine analyses by Michel Agier in *Les Migrants et Nous: Comprendre Babel* (Paris: CNRS Éditions, 2016).

yourself to formulate for them—is that they be their
best, fulfill themselves as much as they can. When
such rogues raise their head, they will be subject to
the laws of the soil on which they stand. Without
injustice, without an excess of hatred, without global
stigmatization, without revenge, without xenophobic
rancor. Without exemplarity. The penalty will remain
inscribed in the beauties of Relation.

May Germany remember this and draw her
strength from it!

Welcoming migrants, who come who go who stay
who continue on, welcoming them without demands,
is to honor a future within them. To trust them with
their own future. Relation assigns no fixity, sem-
blance, or resemblance, no intangible and therefore
fictive difference. No obligatory ancestor. It makes do
with separations, distortions, or fertile divergences.
It does not fear the unforeseeable. Relation is what
instills in multiculturalism the "trans-" of open living
together.

*   *   *

A multi-*trans*-cultural living together.

In our days, every culture is plunged into the world. Every culture is therefore, at intensities that result from its experience alone, multi-*trans*-cultural. Whether consciously or not, Relation deterritorializes. In our individual or collective imaginaries it creates "Sensible Places" that are superimposed on the sensible places of the world. The experience of the world that every individual lives (one's *ingenium,* as the philosophers say) accrues within, enriches the individual's memory, solidifies a "World-Place" that belongs only to that individual: a precipitate of landscapes, music, dances, works, images, and encounters . . . that form a sensible matter in the concrete and the virtual. These "Places" unfold in imaginaries, decide on journeys, link up, "connect" in the end. Spread out across former Territories, Nations, Homelands. Surpass them in one way or another. Magnetic, erratic, with neither inside nor outside, with no established borders, they are a multi-*trans*-cultural evolution . . . They testify, on every occasion in a singular way, to this *global trans-proximity* that our era is experiencing. A great poet of Relation will thus have at his disposal a "cordial geography"; he will be able to come up with his own composite country, his archipelago-country, in the substance of the world and inhabit it as he likes, conspicuously or mysteriously. These are the "Places" that will uncover the migrancies to come, and that perhaps give an inkling of the migrancies of the present.

Individual fulfillment, when it exists in Relation, pushes to the Other, pushes toward the Other, propels the impetus of the "trans-" toward all the presences of life. The "trans-" welcomes constellations of difference (separations, divergences, distortions, deviations . . .) and finds in them a brilliant energy. When their fulfillment is not assured, when they do not succeed in constructing their person, individuals turn back toward communitarian absolutes or marginal and sterile egoism. They descend into fundamentalism and the rejection of the world. On the other hand, their fullness (one might say, their trust enlightened by their fear) opens them to solidarities:

cooperations, exchanges, acceptance of opacities . . .
By introducing impoverishment into our imaginaries,
capitalism perverts individuations and eliminates the
perspective of any sort of fullness. It favors selfish
and, to put it bluntly, consumerist withdrawal. This
withdrawal is an absence from the world, unable to
open or to open itself, unable to welcome and therefore go outside itself. Unable, finally, to read and
grasp the world or to let a poetics of the world relate
adventures within it.

The ecosystem of Relation requires at the very least
that we guarantee human dignity: that we provide it the
means to survive and continue its quest, letting it free to
go. That we accompany it as we should, as much as it
requires. The Other's suffering authorizes no projection
organizing its transparency, deciding its dreams, subjecting it to the humiliating rites of the welcomer, thereby
negating in it any distortion or weakness. Whomever
migrancy throws out into fragility remains entirely
what he is. The impetus toward him must leave him
intact. The world is within him, a wealth that does not
restrict him to any sort of immobility but rather opens
for him an unpredictable future in Relation.

In Relation, difference is not a settled fact. Like the feeling of identity, it is a moment of an experience of the world. Relation knows a multitude of paths. Relation sets up more reflections, rebounds, and transitions than rigid fixities. It transforms mental data, emulsifies cultural traces, and establishes only the fluidity of an ever-changing presence-in-the-world in the shimmering of reinterpretations.

When the world is seen as living—open unforeseeable unknowable, subjected to irruptions of the unthinkable—when it is experienced with trust decency and dignity, in the benevolence of globality, it creates in us "All-World." Being possessed by it is what will open to our divinations the world that the migrants foretell.

Relation does not create a community founded on the same narrative—a great singular story, the same ancestors, the same, now intangible identity. It explodes fixities in a shared consciousness, made up of individual consciousnesses brought to an optimal degree of fullness. A consciousness therefore forever in the process of becoming in a swarm of images. This is why it relinks, relays, relates, rallies, allies, and why this movement resembles joy.

The assumption of the person in the individual frees an internal multiplicity that one must also relink, relay, relate . . . Like a flight of luminescences surging from Reason and unreason, from rationalism and intuitions, from our follies and our wisdoms, our knowledge and our mysteries, all forms of love, all energies of sexuality. Therefore, it is not in the "me-I" contraction that a person discovers his or her unity, but in the fluctuating alliance of the person's internal multiplicities. One used to achieve peace and interior unity through dissolution into a form of uniqueness— my name, my tradition, my god, my identity, my skin . . . Personal expression reinforced only the dominating and civilizing "we." Today, personal expression conveys only the adventure of a singular construction. Solitary without a cure. And solidary in the fulfillment of its high solitude.

This is what I'm trying awkwardly to assert here: migrancies are one of the forces of Relation. They are essential to the relational health of the world.

The Otherness to Be Lived

No strangeness, no stranger, in Relation. Distances
diminish and are moving toward disappearance.
Exile no longer truly exists. Diasporas burgeon and
become rhizomes in metasporas in which all sorts of
citizenships gather. Cultures, religions, languages—
of origin but also all the others—are no longer invisible straitjackets that one must haul around for life.
All of us retain what we like, what we can, what our
mere experience in the world favors on the one hand
or refuses on the other. They have become relational
dynamics that traverse us and that others traverse
with their own dynamics. Placing-in-Relation sweeps
us away one by one and continuously transforms us.
The old otherness—aggressive, terrifying—has no
more space. Images of the Other, sensations, the feel
and the virtuality of the Other, and the world's other
are within us. Arriving, encountering, discovering

is always in part to find again, to *recognize*. All that
subsists, in an imagination practiced in the Open, are
relational proximities, waves that connect. Differences that no longer are absolutes but sudden surges.
Experiences that cross or have crossed paths, and
from crossing paths recognize one another, attract
and repel one another, thus move, mix in the concrete
or on screen, meet or do not meet in any sort of way.
When I say Syria, Iraq, Sudan, Eritrea, or wherever
else, I'm not stating an essentialization. I'm merely
indicating an original impulse, the beginnings of a
more than ever individual experience of a future in
Relation.

No migrant transports a country, a culture, an
absolute language, a complete religion. Only the
combinations useful to his or her survival: the alchemy of globality from which his or her vision
drinks. These combinations circulate from individual
experience to individual experience, without one
being identical to the other. Therefore, in Relation,
we are always new to the Other, and the Other is
always new to us. The progressive experience which
is henceforth the Other cannot be elucidated once and

for all, identified at the outset or beforehand. It is to
be discovered, often to be assessed. Not to be clarified
but to be lived just as it is, in Relation. Your difference, your experience, is not something that threatens
me. It is the movement of another future from which
I can draw (or refuse to draw) part of my own future.
It's good, dear Jane, that in their shadows you saw
eternal roads and graves without address. You saw this
movement.

Wandering That Gives Direction

In Relation, no one today can be confined to a nation, a homeland, a territory, a border, a fixed identity, a national history, ancestors, heroes . . . These ancient marvels can henceforth serve only as a form of self-indulgence. All of us, no matter where we're from, where we're going, will be able to recognize ourselves in them or not, take them in or not, come and go, making a shared treasure of the shadows and marvels of human adventure. Every old nation confronts this beautiful challenge: to create for itself a radiance in which the most decisive force of Relation can be mobilized, one that offers itself up to desires, creates a thirst for knowledge, for protecting or for saving what there is to protect or to save.

We are the guardians of everything.

*   *   *

We are guardians in the name of all and we are guardians for all.

National wealth is destined to be protected by all or by anyone, at the mercy of what comes, what goes, at the mercy of experiences. If national wealth were only to be defended by its citizens it wouldn't have the slightest chance of survival in the relational movement. In Relation, those who close doors and windows, or set themselves up as an absolute, vertical, integrating, and assimilationist power, undoubtedly asphyxiate what they would like to save. Those who open, attract, and offer their treasures to the relational sensibility of all, make the world not only their abode but their shield, their guardian, and the most exact measure of their wealth. No one is surprised that thousands of people want to jump over the City of Lights, forget about the land of the Rights of Man to go straight to England or Germany. Their particular vision of the world can explain such disdain. But I fear something worse: the waning attractiveness of one of the most admirable aspects of France.

The Right to Poetics

A relational ecosystem gives rise to multi-attraction. The movements of the world will no longer, as they do today, go from poverty toward wealth, from the dominated to the dominating, from war to tranquillity, from penury to affluence. They will trigger a cartography of erratic desires, the unforeseeable stimulations of the unknown, of strangeness, of the possible or of the impossible.

A *sentimography* of globality.

These authorized and, all things told, *organized* movements will, better than any global institution, spread wealth, split up poverties, balance penuries, and in the end break with absurd accumulations. Equity, moderation, stigmatization of indecent wealth will be achieved by the flows of globality—the panoramic feeling they offer—as much as by the rights that will arise sooner or later from this other imaginary of the world. In the pantheon of great consecrated rights let us inscribe a *right to the poetics of living,* and moreover to the poetics of globality and Relation. It's like throwing a handful of benevolent forces into the chaos of brute forces.

In Relation, difference is without an absolute reference: at the same time permanent, changing, and dynamic. Thus, it reconnects in our imaginary with the energy of life.

Aestheticizing the Way

The impact of the migrants clashes head-on with our old measures aiming to guarantee the dignity of all. Human rights, like humanitarian and compassionate references, must be activated with all haste. Helpful organizations as well as virtuous charities are also admissible because of the urgency of the thousands of dead.

But the essential allows us a tutelary urgency.

Establishing a new ark of representations.

Invigorating another vision of the world and its future.

This requires the divination of forces that work tirelessly day after day in the invisible, and that are the only ones to hold, if not a solution (here only the most human position possible is profitable from the start), then a route from which luminescent developments will take off, still out of reach of this twilight moment of our imaginaries.

Walls are in our heads and impose their horizons on us.

They blind us to so many perspectives.

The photo of little Aylan had splattered the walls of the world with the possibility of a route. It scintillated for a moment in mental systems closed in on themselves. It unleashed individual or state innovations in certain parts of Europe. But the interest was quickly exhausted, leaving the general wall of Europe with only a few cracks that were filled right away with barbed wire and watchdogs.

So this is what we need to remember:
An image.
A look.
A vision.

*   *   *

In the end the surge of a "presence" that expresses—the vision of the photographer, of course, but also the child forever asleep in the sand—can allow us to sense within ourselves, but also beyond walls and beyond impossibilities, the *landscape of another world.*

I tell the one filming: This is the force of an aesthetic fact. We have to recount, we have to sing, we have to dance, frequent fires of color, operas of light, make music, write in unheard-of languages, go digital, rely on gestures and expressions, see and make seen, repeat, repeat, and repeat again, awaiting each time the alas unpredictable brilliance of beauty.

The Open Soul of Borders

Jane, you saw only silhouettes.

Their borders not only keep you from crossing.

They strip you of winds, of the rustling of foliage.

They take from you a part of your humanity, or even tear it all away.

They appear as if highlighted by these human swells that are becoming urgent. They multiply: religious administrative ethnic territorial psychological . . . a torrent of obstacles that curb imaginations. These borders find themselves put to a severe test and therefore tense up. Their alternative is to be corroded by acids or to be sharpened like guillotine blades. The choice has been made to leave them to the inhuman and to put in place the unacceptable. These multiform borders begin to grind flesh hopes and blood, grind them still, and forever, before our eyes. They kill every day and en masse, but they will yield. They will have to yield before an imaginary of the world that reconnects with its own diversity, that makes images in this way, and that therefore injures walls and borders. No enclosure can contest reality, nor can it invalidate the passage of the wind, the flight of birds, the dégagés of the mind and of great emotions. If a border is not an anomaly in a world woven in diversities, then at least no border can consider the world an anomaly.

Among the camps piling up that become jungles, a strange port geography proliferates: shores under surveillance, humiliating and shameful channeling, police checkpoints, chaotic spaces where people are trapped and which never constitute a destination. They make sure that no one ever arrives. They require people to take flight, to take flight again, into nowhere, forever. A chance welcome, a bit of benevolence, can create here and there, for such and such a person, a fortuitous and probably provisional arrival. But for the others, hindered in their momentum, arrivals remain improbable. Like a star that knows only the yearning of an interstellar void. Even if the fantasized destination could be reached, arrival is often impossible. Desires come up against the rigidities of a very ancient reality. The momentum will be forced to feed off the future it can sense, in a furious and deadly immobility. These repeated movements, these more or less admitted wanderings will elaborate a "presence in the world" that, revolutionary, can only go toward a still unpredictable future.

Their desire for a world is so inexhaustible that they can only see its borders—these old seams of a past world. Like a glance that would lose itself on the blinds of a forgotten window, that no longer closes, suspecting that the future is beyond this relic. They—those who will constitute an unbeatable and continued "presence in the world"—will confer another soul on these borders.

Another breath on the shores.

Another density on the fissures and on the channels to nowhere.

*   *   *

They are going to bring them to life simply by the great breath of their passing through. Oxygenize the rifts over here, fill the gaps over there. Smooth out the scars that had cut up the world before their leap.

Absolutes sought to "integrate" immigrants, so as to disintegrate them. Today, above Nations, "Places" will be the attractive configurations in which all people will be free to lead their existence in the world, in *jus soli,* in *jus sanguinis,* in *jus Relationis.* The greatest attractors of Relation will be "Places" where a version of well-being will be offered.

In the Open, applauded by borders!

Camps from Another World

Their usually half-invisible homeless—small silent tribes, vaguely guilty of being what they are, now a decoration among the urban furnishings, an ordinary wound that their system generates like a foam on the brim of each city, who are nothing, not a political cause, not even a humanitarian one, not even a threat to public order, merely the subject of sporadic management so they don't freeze to death—suddenly transmute into a human tide. A flood of human debris from all corners of the world, who intensify what they are, but who unlike them do not keep their heads down, do not die in silence. Debris who demand to be able to live, to cross, to go, to be treated well, who scream it or demonstrate it in strength and in silence. *Those who should be far away but are nevertheless here join those who were so close yet who were not here.* Together, in the same places, the same filth, the

same misery, they reveal the inhumanity of a system
from which they all descend. When camps spring
up, it's because thousands of invisible camps were
already fermenting in the closets of these nations, of
these cities, of these tranquillities, and of these clear
consciences. Camps are nothing more than the specta-
cle of an already ancient inhumanity.

In the camps, they encounter non-places. They
unite with presences arisen from the dungeons of the
world and endure the experience of the relational fact.
They then discover that other brotherhood: that of *a
future that does not establish a new community,* which
is not a village but reveals the treasures of contacts
that allow them to come there, to go farther still, to
exist in a wake whose origin would be lost and whose
arrival will remain improbable. They realize what national straitjackets, sharp and hostile borders, prevent
us from living and considering: *a single planet that
summons us to nothing but solidarity.*

Here it is, our planet, reimagined in the rough draft
of the camps, like a hand of cards that have been re-
shuffled, a sketch, coarse, dense, and illegible, where
they live from the inside with so much suffering but

so many new comforts. Unprecedented adaptations. They already breathe the still violent wind of a common future, the vertiginous absence of elsewhere in the benevolent and grandiose right-here.

I loved this expression from I don't remember which demonstration: "D'ailleurs, nous sommes d'ici!"[1] It's been singing within me for a long time.

---

1. This slogan plays on the expression *d'ailleurs,* which usually means "by the way" but could also be interpreted as two words meaning "from elsewhere." It can therefore be read either as "By the way, we're from here!" or "From elsewhere, we're from here!" [Translators' note.]

Those Who Read into the World

Let's think of those children who have experienced, who still experience this.

They have known the violence of a world that rejects you.

From their parents, they have learned the violence of vital energy that rebels against extinction and connects you to nothing but the worries of living. They have known the "all-giving" and "all-trying" of a leap into the unknown. From camp to camp, from walls to barbed wire, they have known both exhilaration and death, both asphyxiation and oxygen, all the nuances of heat and cold. They have seen the tears of those who came to their aid, have seen ice-cold stares as well. *They have in fact known another way of living and of inhabiting the world.* What we pity in them is

our own misery with which we have tried to negate
their existence, to tolerate their death. What we envy
in them is henceforth what they read into the world,
what the world reads in them, and thus *what we no
longer know about the world and what the world can
no longer read in us.*

Migrancies are part of this globality that we must
implement. Not organizing them, not *reorganizing
everything* with them, assures no sort of protection for
nations. Rather the contrary. It paves the way for an
ethical drought.

We cannot deglobalize humanity.

We cannot kick it out of globality!

With humility, benevolence, poetic bursts, and creativity, we can only organize a planetary multi-trans-cultural comfort. The "trans-" disarms borders, and thereby
re-enchants them. What the migrants live is a single,
very ancient adventure, which still continues: our human
adventure. No human can remain an impassive spectator
or be exonerated from the weight of these sufferings.

*   *   *

There is only one film.

The ending will be the same for all.

Through them, it is always life that comes, that leaps, that crosses, that calls, never death. Going against life is like choosing death, creating suffering, creating death, dying infinitely ourselves. What they are living is not the destiny of a horde, the confusion of a mass, it is individual thrusts that construct "persons" in the emulsion of the world. Masses scatter, people remain. Their experiences add up and are part of the world. Shape it, build it. Only a policy of care brought to individuals, allowing them all to construct a radiant person for themselves in the great unfolded fabric of the world, will favor efficient global regulations, which in turn will take care of the quality of trans-societal connections, of the preservation of common goods, beginning with our small planet. Only a policy of care brought to individuals will somewhat be able to perceive this other imaginary.

The election of Mr. Trump began with the first migrant shipwrecked with his family in a sea of indifference. It continued in the course of the thousands of deaths that punctuate our months and our weeks. This more or less sums everything up: frustrations, poverty, and miseries that lash out at the mind. The desperation in the assault on borders can in a different context assail the polls, stripe the democratic sky with irrationality. If societies, institutions, states, levels of consciousness, unprecedented intensities of communication are capable of accepting migrant catastrophes, it's because the unacceptable already thrives in their daily lives. There are bits of Trump in each one of us, to a greater or lesser extent, of a more or less virulent sort. Trump is there, in one way or another, in what we accept and what we remain indifferent to, or what seems normal to us. In our usual cowardice, our small shadows that accumulate. If Trump emerges on all horizons, it's because he was already lying in wait within us. It would be wrong to think that we are different from those who voted for him. What separates us is often nothing more than a variation of intensity in our disillusionments, or in the alchemy of our frustration. In the current imperial reign, it's not only miseries that are being established, precarities that are being institutionalized, it's also ethical regressions that exacerbate the despair of sealed horizons. It's also the instinctive lurches of the media, the erosion of political parties that claim to promote common goods and social progress. It's the invalidation of any alternative in the impoverishment of political programs—of their thought, of their courage—beginning with the people who create them for us. It's the growing weakness of states when challenges require a united will and readiness for big decisions. Capitalism is so protean and destructive that it will survive for a long time, even in an empire of ruins. Not only the ruins of an ancient society, but those of the noblest foundations of the mind. When these foundations are annihilated, the ruins become abysses. The triumph of capitalism will resound like a death knell without a steeple and will crumble into I don't know what, on the very base of its victory.

Therefore, all struggles are linked.

Everyone is so to speak a "refugee" in everyone else.

*   *   *

One and the same dependence binds us together.

Our fullness is made of the fullness of unknown people who nevertheless are within us.

All the unknown of the world sustains what we know, brings it to life, determines it too.

Solidarity is necessary as a principle.

For every national sovereignty.

For every individual.

An ardent and multiform solidarity.

Migratory camps are places where something in us withers, where something else in us begins to move toward something else.

Our strength and our weakness are there.

*   *   *

An immense weakness, a stammering strength.

Being conscious of it, considering this strength and
this weakness together, bringing them together as a form
of grace, transmuting them into Relation. No one drew
a relational lesson from the slave trade; the door was
then opened to genocides of Hereros and Namas, to Nazi
camps, to Gulags, to colonial carnages, to executions of
anticolonialists. A loss of vigilance, if only for a second,
brings about an eruption of shrieking unthinkables.

So, Hind is right:

Filming these daily attacks on humanity that seem
marginal to us, so far from what matters to us.

Jane is right:

Offering breakfasts with swirling images of a
humanity reaffirmed in relational benevolence.

Considering that every life is an impetus toward
every other life. That every life can only take care of
life. Remaining sensitive to the humblest and most
luminous that the idea of humanity, the name *humanity,* has to offer. A bit like Saint-Exupéry, who looked

down from his airplane during his night flights on
the archipelago of small lights that made up cities,
villages, hamlets, solitary abodes. Each one of these
lanterns, tiny, buried in the imperial night that covered
both the sky and the earth, became a quintessence of
humanity and filled the poet with emotion. Each one
was a concentrate of hopes, of dreams, of achieve-
ments, of projects and of accomplishments. Each one
lived at the same time of the past and of the future, of
immobility as well as extension without limits. These
archipelagos did not make the night disappear. Neither
on earth nor in the sky. They filled it with gentle poetics. With a dance of permanencies and resolutions that
made of night the beginning of promised dawns and
of inevitable dawns. A grandiose threshold, available
for the illumination of the human spirit as a whole.

Césaire suggested that we never despair, as Creole
peasants often did. Moving down night paths, they
would find themselves surrounded by a flight of
fire-critters that lit up neither the sky nor the earth,
and showed no real path forward. They would cry
out at such times: *The fire-critters only light up their
own bodies!* Césaire would underline to what extent

these small living glows were much more precious
than large floodlights and saving dawns. By their
mere presence, they modified the whole of the night.
Without showing a path, they represented swirling,
insistent, persistent possibilities, as numerous as the
glows, which, in their constant flicker, turned the very
same night into the setting for a future.

Lights and shadows are, from the outset, total.

Each one is the source of the other, its basis, its
impetus.

Each one propagates the other at an intensity
which itself is considerable.

If a glow only touches one person, only stimulates one child, only pierces a bit of the horizon, it's
despite all a victory for a resonance whose wave will
not subside. The election of the blond lunatic was a
night that fell on democracy. But around the world
it lit up a colossal swarm, which shows us that this
night is pregnant with a myriad of futures, while the
half-dawn or half-night that another possibility true to

our blindness would have offered us would not have brought out a single one.

It's the powerful night that compels a powerful dawn.

It's the powerful night that offers the prism of a sun of equal intensity to the images unleashed by the slightest glow.

Yes, my dears, you are right, do not lower your head. Do not close your eyes. Do not defer your desire. Fixate more than ever your eyes upon obscurity while unleashing for yourself, while inventing for all, commas of light.

No pain has borders!

No pain remains an orphan!

No suffering inflicted on the living has a limit within itself.

*   *   *

The victim is within us and the executioner too. Threats unite and affect us together. Each one of us is a target without shelter. A front line and a transmitting antenna. Inaction confers on the slightest indecency a terrible impetus. A child who dies in the Mediterranean recapitulates the ignominies tolerated for millennia by human conscience and accuses us, too. And those who have let him die invoke our name and put us by his bedside as if we were complicit. The slave trade prospered at a level of consciousness nourished by the Enlightenment. Our current level of consciousness, which is that—phenomenal—of a connected consciousness, is infected by the merest cowardice, but it welcomes as forcefully and rapidly a simple refusal, a bit of indignation, an outrage, a smile, a coffee . . . the merest sparkle where vital integrity is protected, and human dignity, like a final torch, sustained.

So, yes, in this night, on this raft, beneath this frozen horizon, among these shivering shelters, camps, and bivouacs, destroyed again and again yet always reconstructed, in Europe, but also in Asia, in Africa, in the lands of the Caribbean and the other Americas, in the unexpected geographies of the wind, in sparks of salt, in sparks of sky, poets and great human beings—Glissant, Pasolini, Edgar Morin, the Mandé hunters, and my François Villon, Georges Didi-Huberman, Césaire, René Char, Perse perhaps far and wide, André Gorz, Derek Walcott, Mahmoud Darwich, García Márquez, my Saint-Exupéry, Mireille Delmas-Marty, Monchoachi, Deleuze, Bacon, Rabelais, Gérard Fromanger, Abdelwahab Meddeb, Miles Davis, Abdellatif Chaouite, Achille Mbembe, Fabienne Brugère, Bruno Guichard, Banksy, Bob Marley, Machado, Moustaki, Kateb Yacine, Frankétienne, Michel Agier, Brassens, Kundera, Montaigne, my Hector Bianciotti, dear Rimbaud, Tagore and Rilke, and so many others and so many others, in sentimography and in sentimenthèque . . .[1]—express their sympathy for journeys that never end, wanderings that reach their destination and nights that light the shores of another world . . .

1. *Sentimenthèque* is a combination of the French words *sentiment* and *bibliothèque* (library). [Translators' note.]

À ceux qui sont tombés avant d'arriver

For the fallen who never arrived

The Poets' Declaration

1. The poets declare: Neither orphan nor without effects, no pain has borders!

2. The poets declare that in the indefiniteness of the universe lies the enigma of our world, that in this enigma lies the mystery of life, that in this mystery palpitates the poetry of humanity: none of these can be dispossessed of the others!

3. The poets declare that the mutual fulfillment of the universe, of the planet, of life and of humanity can only be imagined in a horizontal fullness of life—this way of being in the world by which humanity ceases to be a threat to itself. And to that which exists . . .

4. The poets declare that during the current reign of power, under the iron of its glory, challenges have arisen that threaten our existence on this planet; that, therefore, all that exists that is sensory, living, or

human beneath our sky has the right, the duty to part from it and to contribute in a very human way, or in an even more human way, to its disappearance.

5. The poets declare that coming-going and drifting about the shores of the world are a poetic right—that is, a decency that arises from all known rights whose goal is to protect the most precious part of our humanity; that coming-going and drifting about are an homage offered to those toward whom we go, to those whom we visit, and that it is a celebration of human history to honor the entire earth with its movements and its dreams. Everyone can decide to live this celebration. Everyone can one day be driven to live it or relive it. And all in their strength to act, their power to exist, have the duty to devote the greatest care to it.

6. The poets declare that in the matter of individual or collective migrations, trans-country, trans-nation, and trans-world, no penalty may be imposed on anyone, for anything, and no crime of solidarity may decently exist.

7. The poets declare that racism, xenophobia, homophobia, indifference to the Other who comes who visits who suffers and who calls out are indecencies

that in the history of humanity have opened the way only to exterminations, and therefore that not welcoming, even for good reasons, whoever comes visits suffers and calls out is a criminal act.

8. The poets declare that a security policy that allows for death and that suspends individual freedoms in the name of Public Order contravenes the principle of Safety that alone can guarantee the inalienable indivisible exercise of fundamental rights.

9. The poets declare that a National or Supranational Constitution that would not anticipate welcoming procedures for those who visit come and call out would contravene the Safety of all.

10. The poets declare that no refugee, seeker of asylum, migrant by necessity, voluntary exile, no poetically displaced person can appear in any place in this world without having not one face but all faces, not one heart but all hearts, not one soul but all souls. That they are therefore a product of the Deep History of all our histories, that they therefore incarnate the history of our histories, and consequently become an absolute symbol of human dignity.

11. The poets declare that never again will anyone on this planet have to set foot on a foreign land—every land will be native to all—nor will anyone remain in the margins of citizenship—every citizenship conferring on all its graces—and that citizenship, caring for the world's diversity, cannot decide what cultural luggage and tools it might wish to choose.

12. The poets declare that, whatever the circumstances, a child cannot be born outside of childhood; that childhood is the salt of the earth, the soil of our soil, the blood of all bloods, that childhood is thus everywhere at home, like the breathing of the wind, the salubrity of the storm, the fertility of lightning, always the priority, plenary from the start, and automatically a citizen.

13. The poets declare that the entire Mediterranean is henceforth a place of homage to those who died there, that its shores provide the foundations for a celebratory arch, open to the winds and open to the faintest of lights, spelling out for all the letters of the word *WELCOME,* in every language, in every melody, and that this word plainly constitutes the ethics of the living world.

14. The poets declare that borders only indicate a partition of rhythms and flavors that do not divide but harmonize, that only separate to bring back together, that only distinguish to reunify, and that therefore no watchdog, no smuggler will be able to reign supreme there, no desire will find there a place of suffering.

15. The poets declare that every nation is a Relation-nation, sovereign but solidary, offered to the care of all and responsible for all on the doorstep of its borders.

16. Migrant brothers, who live the world, who live it well before us, brothers from nowhere, O brothers, fallen, unclothed, everywhere retained and detained, the poets declare in your name that the common will against brute forces will feed off minute impulses. That we carry the initiative with us in our ordinary daily lives. That the struggle of every individual is the struggle of all. That the happiness of all flickers in the effort and grace of every individual, drawing for us a world where that which pours and flows over the borders is transformed at that very place, on either side of the walls and of all barriers, *in a hundred times*

a hundred times a hundred million fireflies!—a single one so as to keep hope alive for all, the others to protect the fullness of this beauty from opposing forces.

Paris, Geneva, Guadeloupe, Rio,
Porto Alegre, Cayenne,
La Favorite,
December 2016